Night Rider

MARILYN RICCI

SOUNDSWRITE
PRESS

First published in 2017 by
SOUNDSWRITE PRESS
52 Holmfield Road
Leicester LE2 1SA

www.soundswritepress.co.uk

ISBN: 978-0-9954578-0-5

Copyright © Marilyn Ricci, 2017

Cover image: *Night Rider* by Anne Fishenden

Front cover font IM Fell French Canon.
Fell Types are digitally reproduced by
Igino Marino www.iginomarino.com

Printed and bound by Lightning Source UK Ltd

Thanks are due to the editors of the following publications in which some of the poems, or earlier versions, have appeared: *London Grip, Other Poetry, The Affectionate Punch, Wayfarers, Smiths Knoll, The Interpreter's House, Orbis, Obsessed With Pipework, Magma, Envoi, Soundswrite Anthology* (Soundswrite Press, 2011 and 2015), *A Speaking Silence anthology* (Indigo Dreams, 2013), *Fanfare anthology* (Second Light, 2015), *Over Land, Over Sea anthology* (Five Leaves, 2015), *Under the Radar, The Rialto*.

Twists, Shorthand and a version of *The Picture Palace Tea-Room* were published in the pamphlet *Rebuilding a Number 39*, (Happen*Stance* Press, 2008).

The boy next door was commended in *The Interpreter's House* Open Poetry Competition 2016 judged by Jonathan Edwards.

CONTENTS

Night rider	5
Post-mortem parenting	6
What you left behind	7
Moonwalker	8
Armistice Day, 1964	9
First fridge	10
The joke shop	11
Coming back from the offie on a snowy night	12
Tracing	13

Hannah & Con at Work

Things Hannah worries about at work	15
People Hannah likes at work	16
People Hannah fears at work	17
Hannah at her linking machine	18
Things Hannah likes at work	19
On her own time	20
Why Con hates the perfect binding process	21
Monday in the canteen	22
Folding	23
Offset	24
Trimming	25
Con's life in print	26

The boy next door	27
The Picture Palace Tea-Room	28
Twists	29
Shorthand	30
First flat	31
Small change	32
Late lunch	33
Lunch in the yard of the Hope & Anchor	34
And he can't	35
The wolf and the brooch	36
Philip Marlowe meets his match	37
Soft gown	38
On Rotherslade Beach	39
Momentum	40
Catching the ball	41
Cotton thread	42
The way things often go	43
The end	44
Dancing with Dad in De Montfort Hall	45
This time	46
Watch the roads!	47

Wedi iddo egluro, cododd y Llo ar ei draed. 'Ddis côls ffor ê selibreshyn,' a chododd ei wydr i gynnig llwncdestun i Rhys. Llifodd y gwin, y brandis a phob dim arall weddill y noson.

'Hei, del!' gwaeddodd Rhys ar y rheolwraig. 'Tyrd draw i selibretio efo ni,' a cherddodd hi tuag ato. Roedd hi ar fin estyn cadair ond mynnodd Rhys ei bod yn eistedd ar ei lin. 'Be 'di d'enw di, del?' gofynnodd wedi rhai munudau.

'Cynthia.'

'Wel, Cynthia, mi rydan ni'n mynd i ddod ymlaen yn dda,' meddai wrthi gan ei gwasgu'n dynn â'r fraich nad oedd yn dal gwydr gwin.

'Beth am i ti chwarae chydig o gerddoriaeth i ni? Mae'r dec a'r discs yn y gornel acw,' a chyfeiriodd at un o gorneli tywyll y tŷ bwyta. Cydiodd yn llaw Cynthia a'i thywys i'r gornel. Cafodd help ganddi i roi 'Take the A-train', Duke Ellington, ar y dec. Gadawodd i'r ddisg droi a thywysodd Cynthia i'r llawr. Rhoddodd ei freichiau'n dynn amdani a hithau'r un modd iddo yntau a dechreuodd y ddau symud i guriad y gân.

Teimlai Rhys anadl gynnes Cynthia'n chwythu ar ei war ond teimlai hefyd y brandi'n pwyso ar ei stumog. Mi wellith, meddai wrtho'i hun. Ond wnaeth pethau ddim. Oddeutu bar ola'r gân daeth cynnwys bar y *Café du Nord-ouest* allan o'i stumog. Rhaeadrodd i lawr cefn gwisg goch Cynthia.

Safodd yn ôl a sychodd ei geg â'i law. 'Mae 'na rywbeth yn dda yn Piwc Ellington yn does . . . ?'

Night rider

The steady shush of his bicycle wheel
with its mudguard bent a little too close.
I push back the duvet, look out to see
in flickering streetlamp my father coast
by, flap of his raincoat, framed eyes squint,
pushed along by an unearthly wind;
bike clips glint, like he's in an old movie
and when I wave he salutes his trilby.
There's that ghost of a smile as he pedals
away, not looking back, determined, grim.
Thirty years dead I wish he would settle,
be at peace with himself, make that old frame
stop dead in its tracks, sins forgiven,
let blessed mortality finally reign.

Post-mortem parenting

Since she died, my mother is a better parent.
Don't get me wrong, she was good. But,
whatever the source of a family row, she
placed herself firmly in its eye, raged at
the rising waters, screamed through cartwheeling air
until we prayed our ears would drop off.

These days she's more down to earth,
strokes my hair when my head's in her lap,
calms the searing fires of doubt,
bites her tongue during any fight,
offers a hug when I wake in the night.
At last, breathes life into my failing heart.

What you left behind

Trainers with the shape of your bunions,
seeds for root veg, brassicas and onions,
a slim egg timer with small blue grains,
a broken brolly for inevitable rain,
a silver locket with tiny blurred faces,
six cotton hankies, two pairs of laces,
the keys to the house and garden shed,
the abridged *Jane Eyre* next to your bed,
a Sinclair computer and a floppy disc,
bus pass photo like a terrorist,
several cheap crossword books,
the proverbial trio of flying ducks,
three wooden spoons and a mixing bowl,
Unforgettable by Nat King Cole.

Moonwalker

I walked the moon again last night,
kitted out in my padded suit,
loony boots to keep me grounded,
helmet with its porthole visor,
cords that bind to the mother ship.

What can I say about the moon
that hasn't been said before?

Not much, except I find comfort there,
where my footprints never fade, no air,
bouncing along through empty miles,
no passing seasons to phase me, in fact
the dark side remains   dark,
dusty craters are full of   dust.

Most of all I can just be sad:
touch no base, find no anchor.
Most of all I can just know:
you're not there. Not anywhere.

Armistice Day, 1964

At the kitchen table Dad reads the *News of the World*.
I march in, pull off my Girls' Life Brigade cap:
A whole box of poppies went missing!

My sister talks of catching our death,
Mum plates up roast beef.
And we sit, in silence, and eat.

Sixty thousand, Dad's voice breaks,
tears drip from his chin, expand
on his trousers, melt into the fabric.

Mum sighs, puts down her fork, knife,
my sister turns her head away.
In just one day, he says, almost choking on the beef.

First fridge

The door gasps
light flicks on
cool white box
white wire shelves.
We've never had it so good.

Top compartment
for Birds Eye who tell
us fish have fingers.
The future here for all to see.

Below, a plastic basket
pictures of vegetables
in case we don't know
what's good for us –
and maybe we don't

mistaking white things
for tips of icebergs
cool food for
equal shares.

The joke shop

Wasn't funny. Nor was the man who ran it.
He wore a small plastic spade on his head,
insisted the kids call him Doug.

Then, wearing a red and white clown mask,
he robbed the local Co-op. No one said a word.
Wasn't funny, nor was the man who helped,

wore a seagull on his head, lurked
among the plastic turds, itching powder,
insisted the kids call him Cliff.

Being white, they used comic soap
to colour their hands and face black which
wasn't funny. Nor was the man who killed them.

He wore a policeman's helmet, false nose,
gave each of them a fat exploding cigar,
insisted the kids call him Sir.

Now few people go into the joke shop,
only the mad, the bad and the sad.
Isn't funny. Nor is the cartel who run it.
The main man insists we all call him Don.

Coming back from the offie on a snowy night

In the stark light of the offie,
Mr Robinson sells Dad beer,
barely able to contain a sneer.

Seven bottles clink in our canvas bag,
outside in the clear cold night
Dad's sheepskinned hand holds mine tight.

We spot the Great Bear, Little Bear,
dazzled ground of new laid frost,
our fragile breath made real, lost.

A star shoots. We stop.
Don't tell me your wish,
it'll keep

and on we crunch along the street,
a nipping wind, downy flakes in my face,
already missing his steady pace.

Tracing

The lines are squiggly around Donegal
so my pencil goes slow as I follow the coast
past Dunkineely, St John's Point and on to Killybegs.

Philip O'Riley wanders, peering into inkwells,
half-listening to others bright and beautiful in the hall,
leaving us Catholics alone.

The cliffs of Slieve League are no easier, a tiny tear,
the point squeaks, takes forever to reach past
Belfast and down to the Mountains of Mourne,

then to Dublin and finally Dun Laoghaire.
Philip comes close, leans over: *Teacher's pet*;
while from the hall I hear all things are wise and wonderful,

which somehow reminds me of Saturday night with uncle Mick
and aunty Mary making a holy show, bawling out the songs
in the Emerald Club, though they wouldn't go back, not now.

To my parents, Hannah and Conway.

Hannah & Con at Work

Things Hannah worries about at work

not being at work
work sent back
work which never arrives
piece work
no piece work
going on strike
not going on strike
union subs
no union subs
too much overtime
no overtime
short time
the noise
silence

People Hannah likes at work

Red Elsie, flame-haired, gob
as big as De Montfort Hall, no time
for whiners, slow *wuckers* or bosses
*who think we all floated daan the river
on a packet o' Woodbines yesdeh.*
Helps the women no one else will.

Two machines down, Doreen
flushes to pink when anyone speaks
except on the dinner march home –
My lad's toy train sounds like our machines!
Her dad, back from Burma, not
a single word since.

Betty, on Overlocking, head down,
double chain stitching to stop
any fraying. At home she scrubs
the spotless floors to ease Bill's nerves.
Smokes, alone, as night wears thin.

Hannah at her linking machine

leans in to join
each tiny stitch
to each weeny hook,
straightens the row,
checks the tension,
presses the floor pedal
and the needles go
until sock foot and toe
knit together

on the next row links
Con's open smile back
to his young face, the one
he wore whenever he
chased her, the one
he had before the war

and her mam's heart back
to its strong beat, lungs
to their breath, whole
again, arms to shoulders,
toes to feet

Things Hannah likes at work

Trimming the machines
with paper balls and chains
and crude balloons for wedding days.
Silver keys for twenty firsts.
Babies' bootees for regular births.

Christmas Eve is always best:
swaying tinsel and spiralling twists.
Laughs that start straight after break.
Passing round the under-bench gin.
The blokes next door locking themselves in.

Why Con hates the perfect binding process

Each unit is clamped.
Soft folds are cut.
Roughed up
to absorb the glue
forced into the spine.

The feeder drives
two hard lines
of the backbone.
Nippers pinch
the cover home.

Clamps increase
to squeeze
front, sides, back,
until the unit drops
onto the conveyor belt.

Perfect.
Bound.

Monday in the canteen

Morning break and the headache's fading
though flashbacks still going strong. A cop.
A frown – *You're singing too loud again, Con.*
Hannah's jabbing finger. Worse, her sad sigh.

Couple of fags and hot tea from Glam Vi
who keeps men in line with her tongue.
She shouts at old Ted who brings his own flask.
She'd frogmarch him out for two pins.
Throws his money abaat like a man wi' no limbs.

Jock comes in and she gives him the glad eye.
He asks her out on the usual date. Her lips
curl – *Yer all mouth and no trousers.*
Yer don't fool me, mate. Run a mile if I said yes.
Ach, come on, he says, *just ae fond kiss.*

Keep busy, keep working, keep duckin' 'n' divin'
till the queasy belly and that shrivelled feeling
disappear in the tick of the print room clock.
Rebel songs and mad dreams fold into routine,
swallowed, swallowed by the stamp of machines.

Folding

In Folding the women's deft hands work fast.
There's one whose eyes follow Con cutting through.
After a bad week he's sometimes tempted
to return that look and test its promise.
But he's seen before the crease of a shy smile
turn into a furrow. He's seen a line
of broken men and lost women
shape a card house and believe it strong.
So he keeps on walking into Trimming
where Doug The Blade narrows an eye
and insists all margins are chopped to size.

Offset

You need to make a good first impression.
If that initial sheet of paper is right, you're on.

> *Hannah   clean dress of poppies on white*
> *Con makes her laugh on a one-pedalled bike*

On the metal plate the image attracts ink,
repels water which clings to the free space.

> *Her jet-black curls in full swing*
> *pushes him stronger than he expects*

To prolong the life of the plate, the paper has no
direct contact with it. The image is offset to a blanket.

> *The park   jam sandwiches   bottle of beer*
> *Con strokes her hand her hand her hand*

The paper is squeezed between the blanket roller
and the impression cylinder.

> *Con's frayed cuffs   Hannah's stiffness*
> *Her father's critical eye*

Like similar processes, the final image
is a reverse of the original.

> *Straight-backed in the churchyard*
> *crumpled suit   train of her dress like a pool of milk*

The whole process is based on the fact
that oil and water do not mix.

Trimming

All profit hangs on Doug The Blade
and his team of knife-eyed men.
No place here for margin of error.
Every bleed's cut straight and square.

After the water, ink and sleek rollers,
the blade descends and fixes borders.

Con's life in print

font

pictures
letters
character

impress
shot
run
imprint

in print
press
reprint
press
reprint

out of print
still

***

The boy next door

It might have all held together
if only he'd taken his time.

The pram wheels, one at each corner,
string knotted to the front axle,

soapbox for a seat, might not
have gradually drifted apart

as we crested Saffron Hill,

my legs might not have parted,
the brake not come off in my hand.

I knew it was over even before
the bottom of the hill raced to meet us.

The Picture Palace Tea-Room

Outside rain taps the windows,
blurs the signs. The waitress brings
stainless pots, milk, steaming jugs,
plates of fancies.

The young woman chooses meringue,
nibbles into crisp snow, her first lipstick
pink on white – struggling
to keep it intact. Suspenders pinch.

In the smoky dark below, Cliff sets out
for his Summer Holiday – again,
leaning out of a double decker,
waving goodbye.

The young man adjusts his tie, watches
the waitress in her skimpy apron,
half an ear to his mother who thought
the B film far better. He can smell
damp hair, sees the girl with fresh
cream on her lips.

Downstairs, Cliff leaps off the bus,
cartwheels down the road.

Twists

The night before I'm due to leave,
we hug ourselves at the bonfire.
Flames shoot out like eager hands.
Branches snap. Green shrubs hiss.
Through a twist of smoke I meet
my father's eyes.
Still running through war-torn France.
Eyes that can scarcely believe
a daughter is here.
So bound not to happen.
The wind tightens his coat.
I slip my hand through his arm.

Shorthand

She's come straight from work where she's
learning shorthand. He, for once,
looks unsure

in his overalls, straight from work, speaking
to the salesman who follows the line
of his finger.

She follows the line of his finger to a settee
that might well be a floral tribute
to his mother.

She, for once, is sure. Goes straight to
a gold-fleck moquette, strokes it, leaving
the line of her finger.

I prefer this, she says. He smiles, turns
away. They've come straight from work.
She's learning shorthand.

First flat

Cramped, damp, just married.
Not much room to dream,
a creaking ceiling, one-bar fire.
No place to create.

But we did: endless
washing, sterile bottles.

You left long before the click of the lock.

Never fancied I'd return
but, last night, I did:
and you were there, my love,
sad, angry, at our window,
clamouring for attention.

This time I ignored you,
danced down the hall,
leapt up the stairs, flung open
our door, slid the sash high,
turned to find
you'd left me, again.

Small change

There they are – the crumpled receipts, stray screws,
                                            small change
and your wedding ring – on the side of the bath after
                                                    your nightly shower.

Usually, I dump the receipts and screws in the bin, take
                                              the small change
and place the ring on your bedside table.

Tomorrow, without thinking, you will replace it on your finger,
breeze downstairs, straight out to the shed, not bothering
                                                      to say hello.

There they are – scrumpled little mess and your ring.
I scoop them up: plop, plop into oval porcelain.

After the first flush, only a couple of screws and the ring remain.

People Hannah fears at work

Renee, the supervisor, who never cracks a smile.
Arthur, one of the knitters, who thinks he's a right
to block the entrance to the ladies' lav,
where Rita and Shirley are having a drag,
and Pearl'll be in there, roaring again,
'cos her Cynthia's gone and done it again.
The lad in the office who seems a bit mental,
looks down his nose as if there's a bad smell
coming off the Linkers with their soaring
high windows, polythene for doors; and
Alf, the foreman, who scratches his crotch,
standing behind Doris studying his watch
and Doris speeding up instead of slowing down,
so it's three dozen an hour for half a bleddy crown.

On her own time

no peace in piece work
never enough hours
to make enough money
to spend more time
at home maybe
just on your own
not being watched
for once

Late lunch

My husband grazes in the paddock.
Curious, I approach, wave hello.
He carries on tearing the earth.
Grass soup? I ask. *Your mother's recipe?*
He lifts his head, nods in that way donkeys
do, and I head for the kitchen

past the tack room where I stop, look back at him,
chewing, resentful. I go in. Musk of steed,
leather for broad haunches. At the back
a small saddle made for a dull grey coat, extra
long harness for those ears.

Lunch will be late, I say, tightening the girth,
mounting, kicking on. He refuses, of course.
What's in it for him? Sinks his back legs deep
into mud, rears up those skinny front hooves.
I slide off. Decide to eat out.

The wolf and the brooch

When she wakes the wolf has gone,
taken her magic brooch, her cake.

Following the crumbs she finds him
in his den: up on his back legs,
red lamé dress, diamante stilettos,
admiring himself in the glass.

Her brooch glows on his breast.
He looks so happy. She smiles.
The brooch will take care of him.

Lunch in the yard of the Hope & Anchor

A wasp lands on your father's panini,
it's dismissed, like a silly idea.

Two appear on your beef sandwich,
you ignore them, take a bite.

Their source is a dark hole in the eaves:
frantic, fevered, driven.

Three explore your mother's cheese roll.
Furtively, she turns the plate, round and round.

Four perform high-wire feats on the edge
of our daughter's glass of Coke. She cries.

I take her hand and we move
to a table on the far side of the yard

where we watch you, your mother, your father,
eating lunch in a haze of flight.

And he can't

find the words, can't say
them if he can, sees he's losing
her afraid

the thread will disappear
forever and he can't hold
her, can't locate

the feelings, the thread,
when she looks puzzled
only has

the instinct,
the inkling
of something vital
to say.

Philip Marlowe meets his match

The dame's swimming: powerful overarm
strokes, leaving barely a ripple on the blue
pool in the hard California sunshine.

She doesn't look like a killer, but this is 1930s
Hollywood so every broad's a suspect. Every
man, who's a real man, distrusts what he sees,

and maybe this dame, slicing the water like a hot
knife through butter, is different. Maybe she's
got what it takes to squeeze the juice out of a guy,

like Marty squeezes oranges over on Sunset.
Maybe she's the real McCoy, ready
to squash a PI like a fly on the remains

of her banana split. Maybe it's time he left
this scene before he makes a jackass of himself
to a woman with a powerful overarm stroke.

Soft gown

Child, put on this nightgown I have made for you,
feel its smooth cotton, silky ribbons, embroidered sheep,
let it cradle you through your sleep.

Promise me each night when you are grown,
you will wear a soft gown, lie down as if
to die and ask: *What was vital?*

On Rotherslade Beach

He hauls himself to the next level.
Those rocks are slippery, watch your footing,
her voice carries across the sands.

He waves an arm, not looking back,
grips the rock above with both hands,
hauls himself to the next level.

The sea insists against the rocks,
she sits down, shades her eyes,
her voice carries across the sands:

That's far enough, you're climbing too high,
allows glittering sand to flow through her fingers.
He hauls himself to the next level.

The sea crashes in, sucks back.
How does the world look from there?
Her voice carries across the sands.

He tightropes across a jagged mountain range,
picking his way from the sea, the land, then
hauls himself to the next level.
Her voice carries across the sands.

Momentum

A wild child
runs through the house
pushes over vases
kicks at chairs
up the stairs
into my room where
breathing hard
she jumps on the spot:
I flee! I flee!
then *Wheeeeee!*
down the bannister
out the front door
back over the fields
a receding dot...

Catching the ball

My feet press into shingle, skeletons
of tiny crabs, mother-of-pearl shells.

The early evening breeze brings your laughter,
joyful squeals of your kids.

I've been here before, praying for you to be happy.
Once, in early mist, almost believed it would never happen.

But there you are: vein of scarlet sun behind you,
arms stretched high, feet off the sand, catching the ball.

Stones, skeletons, shells constantly re-shape.
I fling out my arms, turn full circle, blow a kiss to the sea.

Cotton thread

Here you are, sauntering from the park,
waving goodbye to your friend at the corner,
checking your tight, black curls in the newsagent's window;
back to my cottage where you show me a loose cotton thread
on your High School Musical T-shirt. You pull it.
No! I say. *It'll fall apart.*
You giggle, share the thread with me – *Pull it, Nan.*
And I do. And we laugh as a whole seam unravels.

You and I holding a thread so easily broken –
there you are, wearing a crimson headscarf, carrying
a big blue bowl of mangoes on your head, strong
legs rolling beneath you, arms pushing you on
down a white dusty road, brown eyes fixed
on another grandmother's home.

The way things often go

Six a.m. and he's sweeping up after the night shift,
thinking of his finger tracing high cheekbones, warm lips,
hands running through her brown curls
at the bus stop next to the Palais de Danse.

God knows it's been a hard walk against the wind
since that first shy meeting: sucking a mint to hide beery
breath, holding open the door, the apple smell of her perfume
as she high-heels onto red carpet covered in dead ends,
plaster cupids looking down on them.

Later, he wants another drink, she's a little edgy.
The last bus still half an hour away they linger
in the smell of frying chips, joke with the old man
behind the counter, stroll towards the stop, sharing
the chips, the vinegar soaking the paper apart.
He goes to kiss her. She flashes: *Not yet.* Pushes him.

It's an old story, he thinks: early whiffs of fatal flaws –
his drinking, her temper – the inevitable cracks, split.
But it wasn't like that.

He has loved her and, he thinks, she has loved him and that
                                                        endured
through the kids, the arguing, his drinking, her temper, the lack
of jobs, the constant worry about paying the rent.

It's an old story about dead ends, plaster cupids, chips, vinegar
                                                        and love.
An old story about the way things often go.

The end

Your last boy's summer.
You dive from the Odeon,
squint at the screen of sun.
Across the road, Nancy drifts into focus.
You grin. She giggles.
You race the High Street,
swerve into Memorial Park.

The grassy mound smells sweet
as you roll down, arms wrapped tight.
You rescue Nancy from a flame-filled house, car, boat,
drink her hot breath. She blows you a kiss
from a balcony, carriage, dock, as you sail towards The End.

Forty years on, cutting through that park,
you pause and see a skinny boy
in knee-length grey soon to be long khaki
dodging sniper fire, fighting to save yourself,
returning to an already-married Nancy,
a job in 'the Print', waiting, waiting,
waiting for the credits.

Dancing with Dad in De Montfort Hall

You turning up like that during Tchaikovsky's Piano
                                        Concerto No. 2 was
a bit of a facer, particularly since I don't usually go to that kind
                                        of thing; and wearing
your soldier's uniform – rough khaki, beret and massive
                                        shiny boots,

not to mention the Brylcreemed hair, small blue eyes and
                                        nicotine-stained fingers reaching
out, asking me to dance as you hover above the pianist, an
                                        amazing bloke called
Simon from Macedonia.

You whirl me over the violins, the cellos, timpani until we come
                                        to rest above
the brass section who are silent at that point; we look down at
                                        our feet and I want to
laugh at the massive boots, our breath merges, until

our feet float up behind us, we grab onto each other's fingertips
                                        and whirl again,
and again – over the piano, violins, cellos, timpani, the brass-neck
                                        of it.
Trust you, turning up like that.

This time
i.m. Hannah

We will go to Thirlmere.
It will be six a m, have rained
in the night so the path smells
of your woollen coat as we press
under your brolly on the way home
from Saturday shopping in town.
The air will dance around us
like the dawn in our garden before
that holiday in Margate. This time,
the birds will insist we link arms,
keep walking until we get to the edge.
There dead leaves will slip onto water
and you will leave me again but,
this time, it will be alright.

Watch the roads!

Girls as one body head for the park.
Towards us a stick-man riding a bike
looks familiar. I move to the heart

of the gang hoping to stay out of sight,
while a van gives bike-man a little toot,
making him wave, sing; he's pie-eyed.

Girls notice and think it all a great hoot,
bike-man presses on, laughing as well,
I look straight ahead, remaining mute

as Dad wobbles by, ringing his bell:
Hello darling, be careful. Watch the roads!
I blush, look away, pretend all is well

until at my side a friend's face glows:
no-one at home ever calls me darling.
You're so lucky, he must love you loads.

Girl-body moves on, long hair swinging.
Behind us the stick-man riding his bike
is my dad, going home, voice still ringing.

Lightning Source UK Ltd.
Milton Keynes UK
UKOW05f0259130717
305206UK00001B/21/P